AJAX

TRAINING SESSIONS

by Jorrit Smink

**Library of Congress
Cataloging - in - Publication Data**

by Jorrit Smink
    Ajax Training Sessions

ISBN No. 1-59164-080-6
Lib. of Congress Catalog No. 2004093484
© 2004

Editing
Bryan R. Beaver

Printed by
DATA REPRODUCTIONS
Auburn, Michigan

Reedswain Publishing
612 Pughtown Road
Spring City, PA 19475
800.331.5191
www.reedswain.com
info@reedswain.com

Foreword

The day I heard I was going to be the reporter for Het Parool on Ajax Amsterdam was one of the happiest days in my life. Not only could I see one of my favorite clubs in action every day, this was also the chance to learn a lot as a soccer coach, since I had to watch every practice of the team.

I expected to see a lot of difficult drills, in which players had to think, but nothing seemed further from the truth. Ronald Koeman used very easy drills; he loved working on the technique of the players and never did anything too complex. The funny thing was that even though the drills seemed easy, the players still had to think a lot about what they were doing. But they had to think about the tactics instead of trying to understand the drill. Because I was lucky enough to experience a lot of coaching moments and because I am a soccer coach myself, I started to experiment with a lot of the drills during my own practices.

It was a big success. Players loved most drills, and knowing that Ajax also used these drills made everything even more enjoyable. That's why I started to write down all the drills I saw at Ajax and this is the result of that. Most drills can be used at all levels and some I translated to easier levels.

I wish you good luck on coaching and I am very sure this book will help you out. Also, I want to especially thank Ronald Koeman, who allowed me to publish everything.

Jorrit Smink

Director of Youth development SV Ouderkerk,
Head coach of Abcoude A1 (U-19).

INTRODUCTION

A regular week at Ajax

Before telling you what an Ajax practice looks like, it's interesting to see what a week at Ajax is like. Whoever thinks that soccer players are lazy has got it totally wrong. Players of Ajax Amsterdam typically only have one or two days off during a month. Okay, their working days are a little bit shorter than yours, but a soccer player cannot take a short vacation. It's soccer, soccer, soccer, until the season is over.

Ajax usually plays league matches on Sunday. This means an easy practice on Monday. The players who played (most of) the match on Sunday get the easy practice. It consists of a little bit of jogging, some passing and mostly lots of fun. However, the players that did not play on Sunday get a tough practice. So tough that it has to simulate a match. Monday is also the day the second team (B-team or Young Ajax) plays. If a player who didn't play on Sunday is lucky, he can join this team and skip the tough practice.

Tuesday is preparation day for the Champions League. If there is no Champions League, Tuesday is the day off, but as most of you know, Ajax didn't have many days off, because they reached the quarter finals of the European Cup tournament. This is also an easy practice.

Like I said, Wednesday is a match day. And if there is no Champions League match, there could be Dutch Cup matches or matches for the national team. There is almost always some kind of match for most players.

Thursday is again a day for recovering, just like Monday. On Friday preparation for the next league match starts. There are usually lots of games of 11 v 11 on Friday. But these games don't last long and players get plenty of time to rest.

Saturday is like Friday. However, now the team gets some more specialized drills and a lot of system training or training on corner kicks, free kicks, etc. This is again a very easy training session.

Sunday is another match day and after that the week starts over again.

As you can see, most of the practices during the season can't be tough, simply because there are too many matches. So the tough practices are all scheduled during the season's preparation and the short period after the winter break. Also the Wednesday practice on a week without a midweek match can be strenuous.

But what is tough? A practice at Ajax hardly takes one and a half hours. Normally practice starts at 10:30 am, but last year the team always arrived late on the pitch. It was not unusual for practice to start at 10:40 (though practice may have started earlier in the dressing room with a speech by Koeman or one of the other coaches). Practices always ended at noon.

Every practice started with a warm-up by Laszlo Jambor. This normally took ten to fifteen minutes, depending on the program of the practice and on whether there had been a match the day before. After this warm-up, the team would usually continue with one of the shooting and passing drills. After this there would be time for either a match or another drill, depending on the day. Thursday, for instance, was usually a day with lots of shooting. After this specified drill, you'd probably think it was match time. But Koeman mostly avoided matches at the end of practice, especially at the end of the season.

As you will notice with the drills, a ball is used in all Ajax practices. However, there were some running drills that didn't use a ball. I did not include these drills in this book, because they were only used during the pre-season and because coaches of non professional teams usually don't have the time to implement them.

I also did not write down all the different training matches that were played. Everything from 4 v 4 to 11 v 11 was played during the year. Remarkably, it was rare for the team to play games with uneven numbers (7 v 6 or 5 v 4). Games were always played with the same amount of players on each side. I also did not write down the drills that were overly specialized, like the ones before matches against Arsenal and Feyenoord. Koeman normally did not use more than four drills during one practice, choosing to do several repetitions of each drill.

About the system(s)

Depending on the strength of the opponent, Ajax could choose between two different systems. In the national league Koeman often chose for an offensive system, while the he played a little more defensively in European Cup ties. Especially in European away games you can say Ajax played on the counter-attack. The systems might help you to understand the drills and the why the coaches chose them.

There were many similarities between the two systems. Both involved a flat back four, with preferably one left footed (Cristian Chivu, 4) and one right footed (Petri Pasanen, 3) player at the heart of the defense. The two full backs (Hatem Trabelsi, 2, at the right and John O'Brien, 5 or Maxwell, at the left) played as big a role in the offense as possible.

Where the central defenders were only allowed to attack during free kicks or corner kicks, the outside backs had to support the wingers or even go past the wingers to make the cross themselves. Tunisian star Hatem Trabelsi has developed into one of the best backs in the world. With his speed he is a threat to many a defense, while he also has enough power to play a role in the attack during the whole ninety minutes.

The backs have the space to come up because the two (defensive) mid-fielders mostly play to the center of the midfield. One of those midfield-ers (6 or 8) is always allowed to support the offense, while the other one has to support the defense the moment Ajax loses possession of the ball. They are never allowed to attack at the same time. Rafael van der Vaart, who comes from the left, is the offensive midfielder in most cases, while Tomas Galasek has a more defensive role.

The number 10 is for the offensive midfielder (often Steven Pienaar, but Koeman made many changes during the season, Van der Vaart and of course Jari Litmanen also played at this position for instance). The role of the number 10 is a difficult one. He has to play 'off the ball', so he is not in possession of the ball much. His job is to be in the right place at the right time, which means he has to score! He is often the final station, the finish-ing station.

That's also the reason why many strikers (9) have a lot of difficulties when they join Ajax. Their role is not only to score, but also to build an attack.

9

Very often they are one of the first stations of the attack and they have to keep possession of the ball until the midfielders are ready. Then they can make a choice which way they want to go.

The wingers (7 and 11) have an easier task. They have to stay wide as soon as the ball comes near and they have to be sure to send in a lot of crosses. Since Koeman has become coach at Ajax, the wingers send their crosses in at an earlier moment. They do not reach the goal line anymore, but start passing when they reach the edge of the penalty area.

The reason for this is probably that a cross is a moment in soccer in which your team often loses the ball. This means it is a moment of transition. And of course it is much easier to change over if you come from the penalty line than from the goal line.

The transition of Ajax is very good in both situations. They are able to switch to attack in no time (like they did with beautiful goals against Olympique Lyon and Valencia for instance). But most importantly: the moment they lose possession, Ajax is able to reorganize very quickly. Especially in European matches this means the difference between winning and losing. Every player knows his task and is able to switch back.

The biggest difference between the two systems is the moment the opponents are in possession. While Ajax plays with two defensive midfielders in most Dutch league games, they play with only one defensive midfielder in European games. This sounds more offensive, but actually it isn't.

The triangle on the midfield switches from the point forwards to the point backwards. What happens is that the offensive midfielder makes way for an extremely defensive midfielder. He is actually an extra defender, usually defending the number ten of the opponents.

This little change in the system (the other defensive midfielders aren't attacking anymore now...) has a big impact on the way Ajax put pressure on the ball. During Dutch matches Ajax usually put pressure on the opponent very early. Deep in the opponent's half, the wingers and the striker chase the ball, which often ends in a ball being passed back to the opposing goalkeeper, followed by a long ball from the keeper. Since Ajax is now missing one player in midfield however, they have to wait to put pressure on the ball. So they move back to their own half and then start to chase. This way the opponents do not have much space to play in, so it is easier to defend, since Ajax always has several players around the ball in this small area.

Koeman practices a lot on understanding the system with special drills. He plays a lot of matches of 11 v 11. Matches take ten minutes, with a rest of three or five minutes, in which Koeman explains the system. This is why you will not find many specialized system drills in this book. And that's also what makes this book so interesting. Almost all the drills Koeman does can be very easy translated to the situation of your club!

THE EXERCISES

1. Ronald Koeman's famous ("terribly boring") warm-up

Maximum of 12 players

Player A passes the ball to player B, player B receives the ball with his left foot and passes to player C with his right foot. Players rotate after each pass.

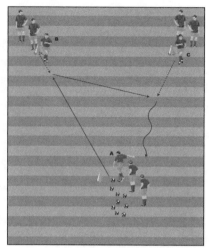

According to Koeman, USA international John O'Brien is one of the players who is excellent in this drill that is all about passing and very good for all levels and ages.

The drill is all about receiving and passing with the correct foot and with the correct speed. Also player C has to call for the ball at the proper moment (just before B receives the ball).

The drill can be made more difficult in different ways. Player B, for instance, can first wall pass the ball back to player A, move away from the ball, receive it and then pass it to player C.

Of course it's very important to use both sides of the triangle for the starting pass to practice both feet.

"They should be able to pass the ball with both feet," Ronald Koeman told me after a practice that started with this drill. "And we will keep on practicing it until they are totally bored. I really don't care."

The players must be bored by now, but Koeman insists on trying to make things perfect and keeps on using the drill.

2. An easy warm-up (or is it?)

5 players

This looks easy, but players find it difficult to decide where to go. It's a warming-up drill and there is no coaching. There is a lot of running involved and a lot of thinking. The drill guarantees your players are into soccer with their minds.

Player A passes the ball to player B. Player B passes the ball to player C. Meanwhile player A has moved to B's spot and B moves to A's spot.
C passes to A, who passes to D. C moves to the central spot, A moves to C's spot, and so on.

The drill helps players to find space and not just to follow their pass.

When young Ajax was hit by a lot of injuries, this drill was one of the favorites of coach John van 't Schip. There were a lot of weeks he worked with just five (!) players.

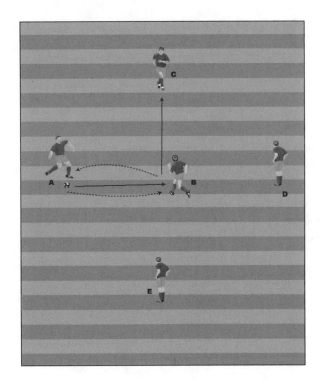

3. A fun warm-up

As many players as needed

In a big square the team plays tag. There is, however, a difference with the normal rules: there are two tagging players, but only one ball. The two tagging players can throw each other the ball. Only the one with the ball can actually tag a player. The objective is to tag as many players as possible in 35-40 seconds.

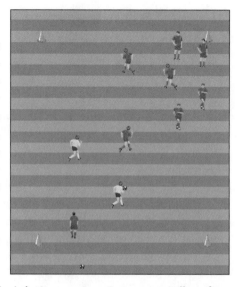

Coach only on spirit and having fun!

Sometimes you need some pure fun during a practice, especially after some tough weeks with hard work or maybe after a disappointing result. This game (most likely one of the many inventions of game specialist Tonny Bruins Slot) is definitely one of them. It might look childish, but all the Ajax players (even the always straight faced Jari Litmanen) have fun during these occasions.

And of course they have the same tricks up their sleeves as little children do. I saw Andy van der Meyde put the ball under his shirt and surprise Steven Pienaar by tagging him. The reaction of the group to this trick was of course exactly the same as when this happens to six year olds: everybody laughed at Pienaar, who tried to act as if he was very angry.

Playing tag with young children is always a good game, especially during a warm-up. You can also play this drill with all the players in possession of a ball, so everybody dribbles around, avoiding the tagging player, who is also dribbling.

4. Just another warm-up

8 or more players

Player A passes to player B, who passes to player C. Player C dribbles back to the position of player A, player B sprints to C's position. Player A rotates to B's place, receives the ball from E and passes to D.

Pass the ball with the left and right foot and coach player B especially. If he wants to turn to player C, he should receive the ball with his left foot and pass it with his right. This should be done in order to keep the ball moving quickly.

A variation on this drill: Player B makes a wall pass to player A, who passes a long ball to player C or D. For this drill it's also very important that B makes a good wall pass and thinks about what direction A wants to pass to. B should pass to the left or right foot with the correct pace.

This drill was mostly used when the players would also have to do a lot of passing and crossing in the second phase of the practice. John van 't Schip, the coach of young Ajax (U-23) and very good at passing the ball himself used it more than Ronald Koeman, who was keener on using his own two warm-up games.

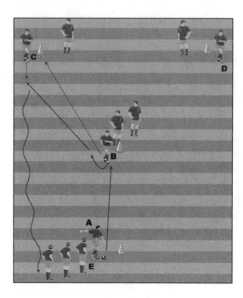

5. Improve the pass with your laces

7+ players

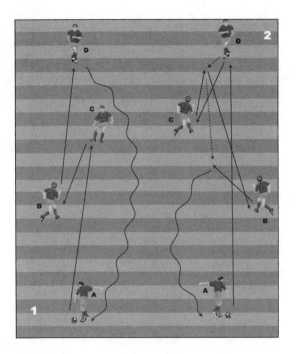

Four players stand in line, 15 yards between each player. There are many different ways to play. I will explain two.

Player A passes to player C. Player C passes back to player B, who passes to player D. Player D dribbles back to the position of player A. Player A becomes player B, player B becomes C and C becomes D. Besides coaching on the pass, you can also coach on the movement without the ball. Players B and C are in line, so there has to be movement. If player B moves to the right, C has to see that and immediately move to the left, so player A can easily reach him.

Player A passes to player D. Player D passes back to player C, who makes a wall pass, then D passes to B and another wall pass follows. D then dribbles to the position of player A. Again, player A becomes B, B becomes C and C becomes D. Now movement without the ball is even more important!

19

If the drill proves to be too difficult, make it easier for your players and make the distance smaller. Also, give a good example. It is easy to tell a player how to shoot, but it is even easier if you can show it as well.

At Ajax, maybe nothing is more important than perfect positional play. Especially when they play in the Dutch league, as opponents then move back (Italian style) and wait for the attackers to make a mistake. To reach the perfect positional play, players have to be able to pass the ball to each other at full speed. Only then can you find that small gap in the defense you need to score a goal.

If you want to play offensive soccer, your passing game needs to be good. And even professional players can always improve. This drill was often used at Ajax, but is also perfect for all ages to learn how to pass or shoot.

So once again:
- Eye on the ball
- Approach from an angle
- If shooting with the right foot, put your left foot next to the ball (too far back will make the ball go up, too far forward will keep the ball low, but you will lose power)
- Point toe of left foot towards the position you want to pass
- Point toe of right foot towards the ground, the moment you shoot
- Point your left arm towards the position you want to pass
- Make contact in the heart of the ball
- Lock your ankle
- Follow through

6. Another extension of the warm-up

7 players

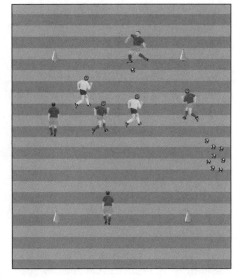

If you are going to do a tough practice, or if your team had some tough days anyway, this drill is an ideal one to start your practice session.

It is just a 5 vs 2 positional play and every player can touch the ball only once. If one of the two defenders wins the ball, he switches places with the player that made the mistake.

Play the game on a small field to make the players warm-up a little and work on their foot skills. And add some fun competition by having the two defenders do push ups if they don't win the ball quickly enough.

At Ajax this game is played by the U-19 team of Danny Blind and lots of other youth teams. The players love it and always have an eye on the chance of nut megging an opponent. There's nothing worse for a Dutch player than to get nut megged. The Dutch word for having a ball played between your legs is PANNA. The whole team always shouts "Panna!" when it happens and there is always a player ready to measure the space between the legs of the player who received the panna.

When that happened to Jari Litmanen (Wamberto did the measuring) he did not laugh anymore for the rest of the training and looked angry. This is not a game for serious Finnish players.

Of course you can also play the drill with other numbers of players.

7. How to shoot?

1 goalkeeper and a maximum of 10 players

Player A passes the ball to player B, who has to shoot on goal immediately. After the shot, player A rotates to B and vice versa. Player B can shoot when the ball is out of the penalty box.

This easy drill (who doesn't know this one?) is all about shooting with your laces. It's about the technique. Players are obliged to shoot with their laces in this drill and are not allowed to use the inside of their foot. What is this about?
- Eye on the ball
- Approach from an angle
- If shooting with right, put your left foot next to the ball (too far back will make the ball go up, too far forward will keep the ball low, but you will lose power)
- Point toe of left foot towards goal
- Point toe of right foot towards the ground, the moment you shoot
- Point your left arm towards goal
- Make contact in the heart of the ball
- Lock your ankle
- Follow through

At Ajax they regularly practice this at all levels. At the start of the season, it once went so badly with the first team that Ruud Krol told them to do push ups every time they shot a ball over (not over the goal, but over the fence behind the goal). It didn't really help, no less than eleven players had to do push ups during the practice and the equipment people had a very tough day.

It's also remarkable to see that someone like Steven Pienaar, who has an outstanding technique, has such a poor shot. I'm always wondering how good he would be if he were able to shoot perfectly with his laces.

8. Koeman's triangle with finishing

9+ players and one goalkeeper

Player A passes the ball to player B, player B passes to player C who receives the ball. He can dribble a little and then finish on goal. Players rotate, so player C becomes A, A becomes B and B becomes C.

This is an extension of Koeman's famous warm-up drill. The only difference is the shot on goal. You should coach like in the warm-up drill, with some extra coaching on shooting.

This game was only played a couple of times on the Ajax pitch, but I used it many times myself, because the warm-up drill can be quite boring. This way, you're able to make it much more interesting for the players. The only problem is that this drill might go too quickly for your goalkeeper. So in my rotation system player C can shoot, but the next player C dribbles back to the position of player A.

9. Shooting and conditioning

3 or 4 players plus 1 goalkeeper

Player 1 makes a wall pass with player 2 and tries to score on goal. After the shot, player 3 immediately makes a wall pass with player 4 and he also tries to score. As soon as he is finished, player 1 starts again with player two, and so on.

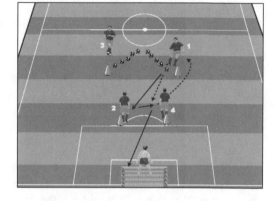

Usually both shooters shoot five balls, then change with the wall passers. To put an extra workload on the shooters, it can also be played with one shooter and two wall passers.

It is of course an ideal drill to work with points to find out who is the best shooter. However, the Ajax coaches did not do that too often. "A good players does not need to be motivated by a point system," Ronald Koeman once said.

This drill is ideal for practicing shooting and conditioning. Mostly it was used during the preparation phase to the season. What makes it an excellent drill is that the it combines both fitness and sharpness in shooting. Players get exhausted during the drill, but still have to manage to score. The difficult part for the coaches is that players try to walk back as easily as possible to give themselves more time to recuperate. At Ajax, striker Nikos Machlas was a star player in easing drills. In the end all the coaches were paying extra attention to him to make sure he did everything the right way (the Ajax way). By the way, Machlas was transferred to Sevilla on loan during winter break.

10. Heading and conditioning

4 players and 1 goalkeeper.

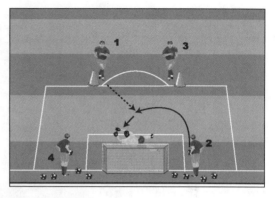

Just like drill number 1, you combine technique with conditioning. This time you work with heading. Players 2 and 4 stand next to one of the goal posts and have five balls each. Player 1 starts at the cone, runs to the 6-yard area and tries to head in the ball that player 2 threw. Immediately player 3 starts while 1 runs back. The game goes on until both players have headed five or six balls and then the headers switch with the throwers.

Coaching is very important, especially to get everybody motivated. At Ajax, second assistant Tonny Bruins Slot is a master at getting the players to run and run, motivating them every second.

To really work on fitness, this drill can be done best about three times in succession, with a one minute rest after the two pairs have headed the five balls.

For Ajax players this is mainly a conditioning drill. But at lower levels, my advice is to pay special attention to the heading technique. The power of a good header comes from the back. Also, good advice for the players is to head the balls to the ground to make it more difficult for goal-keepers.

11. Finishing and conditioning

2-8 players and one goalkeeper

One of the two players in the square calls for a ball from the coach. As soon as he has it, he tries to outplay his opponent and score on goal. If he scores he can call for the ball again. If he misses, the other player calls for it. If, during the 1 vs 1, the ball goes out of play, the player who should have gotten the throw in can call for the ball again.

Match takes 1-2 minutes. After the match, the two players can rest and two new players come in. During the preparation phase to the season, players get a lot of rest and this drill can even be played with 8 players (so players have one minute of action and three minutes rest). The further you get into the season, the fewer players you use, so the rest period is shorter.

Besides the fact that it is once again really important to motivate the players, you can also coach on how to win the ball. First, players have to create space for themselves, then they call for the ball. The best way to do this is to stand behind your defender and then call. It's also important to accept the ball the right way. If possible a player should not have his back to the goal.

Zlatan Ibrahimovic and Jari Litmanen are excellent examples of players who are able to call for the ball at the right moment. They also can hold the ball very easily and have a perfect eye to see when they can outplay the defender and shoot.

12. Conditioning with a fanatical match

6 players and two goalkeepers

Two teams, each consisting of three players and one keeper play a match in the penalty box. There are four quarters of three minutes, since this is, if played fanatically, very intensive. The halftime rest is three minutes or less.

The goalkeepers aren't allowed to score. If the ball goes out of play at one of the sides, the first player to get to the ball can throw in. If the ball passes one of the goal lines, one of the keepers brings a new ball in play.

This is a drill in which conditioning is really important and players should be coached, especially on accuracy. Players have to give everything they have during those three minutes and the coach should motivate them. You can also coach on shooting. Players should shoot as soon as possible. They are in the penalty box! Shoot!

This is an excellent and fun drill for all ages and also a perfect finishing drill.

If you have twelve players and two goalkeepers, make four teams of three and let two teams play, while the other teams do an easy drill with lots of rest.

13. A great conditioning and shooting drill

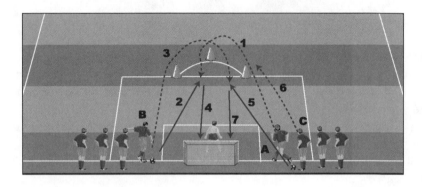

8 players and one goalkeeper

Player A starts sprinting.
Player B passes the ball towards the central cone.
Player B immediately starts sprinting.
Player A tries to score.
Player C passes the ball towards the central cone.
Player C immediately starts sprinting.
Player B tries to score.

Motivate the players! They get really tired. Ajax works with series of about 4 to 5 minutes of action and 3 to 4 minutes of rest.

It is funny to see the effect that fatigue has on shooting technique and accuracy. You will notice that players will find the net easily in the first minute, but shoot wide or especially over at the end of the fifth minute. Ronald Koeman introduced this drill just after Christmas and after seeing that the players liked it, he used this drill at least once every three weeks. It is a perfect conditioning drill, and the players also actually play soccer. You could just let the players sprint, but why not give them the added bonus of a scoring opportunity after the sprint?

14. Heavy work on conditioning in technique

2 or more players

Two players face each other. The distance between them is about 3 to 4 yards. Player A has the ball in his hands. He throws it to player B. Player B returns the ball with his right foot. Player A catches the ball. Meanwhile, player B does knee lifts. After five returns with the right foot, player B becomes the thrower and A the shooter. After another five shots, player A becomes the thrower again and they keep on switching, using a different skill every time:

Right foot inside
Left foot inside
Right foot laces
Left foot laces
Receive with chest, return with left or right foot
Heading
Chest, foot and head back
Chest, knee, foot
Receive with foot and then pass it
Think of many more combinations

Work on this for about 15 to 20 minutes, switch to another drill and then switch back to this drill. The goal is to get the ball back without a bounce.

I tried this drill many times with all different age groups (9-18) and every group absolutely loved it, especially when it was turned into a game. Who makes the fewest mistakes? On a rainy day with a bad field, this is ideal, because you don't need the field at all. With one group we did this the whole practice while players were standing in a field that had more water and mud than grass. We ended with a combination of chest, left knee, left foot, right knee, right foot, another chest, another foot and a header back. Some kids were able to do this five times in a row!

15. Conditioning while passing and shooting

9+ players and two goalkeepers

Goalkeeper A throws the ball to player 1, who passes it to player 3. Player 1 sprints down the line. Meanwhile, player 3 passes the ball to player 2, who makes a wall pass back to player 1. Player 1 sends in the cross and player 3 finishes on goal. Player 1 then becomes player 2, player 2 becomes player 3 and 3 becomes player 1 at the other side of the goal, as this drill is played with two goals.

At Ajax they use this drill especially for building up stamina. However, this drill is also excellent for practicing techniques like sending in crosses, finishing or, for instance, on coaching a full back who helps the attack.

My advice is to use two coaches if you are going to use two goals to play this drill, because the organization can be quite chaotic. It's also possible to use one goal to play this game. In that case, player 3 would just rotate back to the position of player 1.

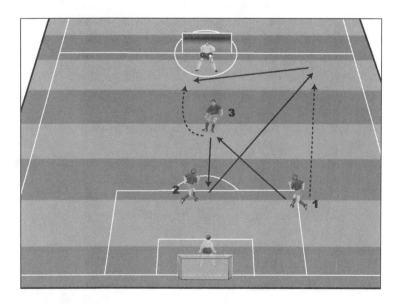

16. Active resting after sprinting

8 or more players and a goalkeeper

One player passes the ball through the air into the square. The player in the square tries to receive the ball and immediately shoot on goal. He is not allowed to let the ball bounce on the ground before shooting on goal.

This drill is designed as a productive activity during the resting period between two sprinting periods. So there's no real fanatical coaching. However, it's nice to see how good the skills of the Ajax players are. This drill is extremely difficult, but many players still manage to score (Zlatan Ibrahimovic especially). It is important that players know how to receive a ball with their chest. Many people think you have to pull your shoulders back while doing this. In fact you pull the shoulders up a little and then push them towards each other. That way you make a little pocket, while at the same time leaning back of course.

This drill is made for skilled Ajax players like Ibrahimovic, Van der Vaart, Pienaar, or Litmanen. To make it easier for your team you can allow them to let the ball bounce or you can take away the square, so they have more space.

17. Passing, dribbling, feinting, scoring! (and defending!)

8 players + 1 goalkeeper

Player A passes the ball to player B. Player B dribbles towards the goal, tries to feint player A and score. If player B scores, or if player A wins the ball, play starts again with two new players.

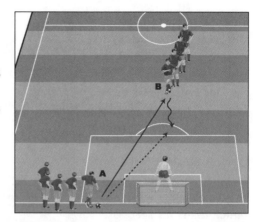

Two important things to coach on with this drill.
The feint itself. There are many types of feints, and players should actually practice them without opposition first to see which feint(s) suits them best. In this drill, the coach explains to the player the proper moment to start the feint. The first requirement is speed. Without speed, a player can not do anything. So you have to coach player B to generate speed. Then he should start the feint at the right moment, which is about 2 or 3 yards away from his opponent (also depending on the feint). After his movement and trick the player accelerates away. In short, the move consists of a burst of speed, the feint, and another burst of speed.

The technique of the defender. A defender should NOT approach the attacker at full speed. He should sneak up to him, while bending a little bit forward and putting most of his weight on the front of the feet. That way he can easily turn if necessary. A defender should always look at the ball and not to the leg movement of the attacker. He should try to get the attacker away from the goal and wait for the correct moment to win it. Let the attacker make the mistake.

At Ajax, coaching was not necessary, they used this drill as a warming-up. Especially at youth level, you can practice this game for hours and hours, it's a perfect learning situation with lots of ball contacts. You might not have expected this easy drill in a book about Ajax, but I think it's interesting to see that even at the top, they still don't forget the basics.

18. Marking an attacker/losing a defender

6 players

The two players in the middle play 1 v. 1 and try to maintain possession of the ball. They can only touch the ball once, just like the four wall players, who the player in possession of the ball can use. The wall players can't pass the ball to each other more than two times in a row. The match takes 45 seconds, followed by a one minute rest. Players rotate.

The player not in possession has to mark his man very closely. Only then will he be able to have a chance to win the ball. The player in possession has to lose his attacker. He has to pick the proper moment for a short sprint to come into the ball, or to sprint away from the ball and his marker. He has to communicate to the wall player in possession where he wants the ball: in his feet, or into space if he wants to sprint away from the ball. The wall players also have to help each other. Eye contact is also a key.

Sometimes Ajax tests players and invites them to the club for short internships of one week. A Japanese and a Brazilian player were the unlucky ones to have to play this game. Both were not able to touch even one ball when playing in the middle against Rafael van der Vaart and Richard Witschge.

To make this drill easier you can allow the wall players to touch the ball twice. That way you're certain they won't make too many mistakes and you will have a lot of coaching moments with movement of the attacker.

19. Improving the cross and finish with a game

12 players and 2 goal keepers

There are three teams of four. One team are the wall passers. The other two play a match. Of course the object is to score as many goals as possible.

This is an ideal game to coach the movement in front of the goal, just before and during the cross. There is always a player running to the near post and one to the far post. These players should not be positioned in one line of the goal. At Ajax, they usually also cross each other and normally those players are the striker and the 'number 10'.

This game can be played in lots of different ways. Even Ajax did that, one time every goal was a point, the next time goals from crosses counted for two. It has also been played with only goals scored from crosses being counted. Usually the winner of the game stays in and the losing team becomes wall passers, so the three teams play a little tournament.

The game is definitely a fun one to play. From my experience, it works at every level and with every age, starting from about eleven years old. You can make it easier by not allowing the defenders to duel with a wall passer, thereby giving the wall passer enough time to give a decent cross.

20. Crossing and choosing position in front of the goal

1 goal keeper and 10-14 players

Player A passes the ball to player B. He opens with a high ball to player C, who was already sprinting. This pass should be with the left foot (or with the right foot if you play it from the other side). Player C dribbles up to the goal line and gives a cross to player D and E. These two players try to score, while there is one defender trying to keep them from scoring.

Even though this drill looks very easy, there are a lot of potential coaching moments. For instance, the moment player B and C call for the ball, or the technique of giving a good cross (come from an angle, finish the shot, etc). Most important at Ajax was the movement of players D and E. They should cross each other and one goes to the near post, while the other moves to the far post. **MOST IMPORTANT: *These two players may never be in one line with the ball!***

When Gerard van der Lem (current coach of Saudi Arabia) was the coach of Young Ajax (the B-team), he used this drill a lot. And with success! The team scored a lot of goals during the season from crosses.

To make it easier, you can of course also play this drill without a defender.

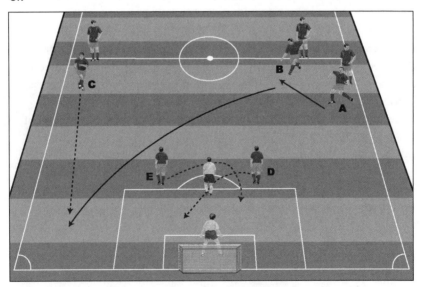

21. Positional Play

12 players

On a field of 20 yards by 40 yards, there is a wall passer on each side. The wall passers can only make real wall passes (therefore not touching the ball twice). The eight players in the middle play 4 vs 4. They try to stay in possession and the wall passers help the team that is in possession of the ball.

Depending on the stage of the season, the matches (I say matches because you can for instance work with points and give a point to each correct wall pass, even

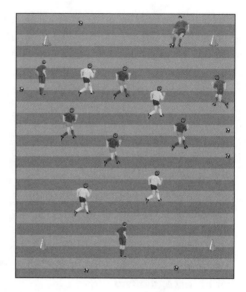

though Ronald Koeman rarely does that) usually take around three or four minutes. After that, one of the teams goes out and becomes wall passers, the wall passers come in and become normal players.

This drill with wall passers is always a players' favorite. There is a lot of action and there's no better feeling than to totally outplay the opposite team. At Ajax the field on which they play this drill is usually not that big. The main goal is usually to lose your personal opponent and then find space. Players like Jari Litmanen and Wesley Sneijder are geniuses in this tactical game.

To make it easier, you can of course make the field bigger, or allow the wall passers to touch the ball twice.

The first time Marco van Basten coached at Ajax, he did this drill. To make the game go quicker he passed in a new ball every time a ball went out of play.

22. Positional play and technique

6 players

It's four against two on a very large pitch, so the players can only touch the ball once. The object of the four players is just to stay in possession as long as possible. The object for the two players is to win the ball. If the two win the ball, they just give it back to the four and the drill starts all over again. If the ball goes out of play, the coach plays in a new ball to one of the four players.

The drill can be played in two different ways. It can be played based on time. For instance the two players in the middle switch after a minute with two other players.

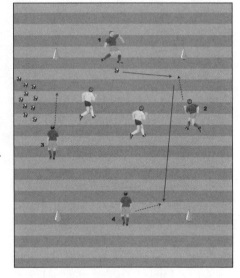

But it can also be played on fouls. For instance, the two players in the middle switch if they have won three balls.

It is very important in this drill to coach players to help each other. If player 1 has the ball, player 2 or (and) player 3 needs to close in to be able to get the ball and open to player 4.

This drill looks like a one hundred percent positional drill. But the practice on technique is also important. Coaches can teach players how to stand the right way (bending over a little) and it's an ideal practice on how to use both feet. You need to be able to shoot left and right in order to make it in modern soccer. This drill is impossible if you are not able to use both feet.

This is very difficult! Even at Ajax, players do not often reach more than ten passes while in possession. To make it easier for your players, you can of course allow them to touch the ball twice.

23. More positional play

9 players

There are three teams of three players. One of the teams starts in the middle as chasers. The other two work together and try to maintain possession of the ball. As soon as the three players in the center win the ball, the team that lost the ball becomes the chasers.

One or two touch maximum. You can also play it based on time. Every team is in the middle for three minutes.

Coach especially on the positional play of the six players. They should open up at the correct moment. They have to make it easier for each other by helping each other. For instance, after player A receives the ball from a long pass, player B and C immediately close in to help him out and to get the ball back to the other side if necessary.

The chasers should never be in one line and they should communicate with each other. Find out what the correct moment is to win the ball. Help each other by chasing in such a way that you force the player in possession of the ball to go to one side.

Coaching the three players in the middle is not easy. It needs insight from the coach, as well as concentration from the players. In general you'll start to coach on communication aspects when players reach the age of fifteen.

24. Finding the third man

10 or 11 players

Two teams of 4 players try to maintain possession of the ball. Both teams can use the two neutral wall players and the sides to do so.
The game is not necessarily played with a points system, but if so, ten correct passes in a row amount to one point. A match takes five or six minutes.

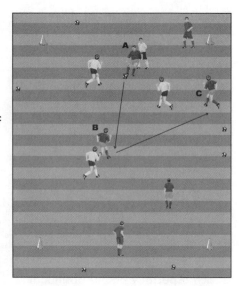

The most important coaching aspect of this drill is the positional play. At Ajax, they coach on finding the third man. To pass the ball around they had to pass it to somebody they were able to see. And that player had to find the free third man.

So, player A should not make the difficult turn to find player C, but he should use player B, to make it easy for the team. If player A would make the turn, he would be searching for something while the solution is much easier: pass it to B, who is able to see both A and C.

The Ajax coaches are big fans of positional games with wall players. And they can be played in many different ways. The drill can also be played with an extra wall player in the center, who tries to move in such a way that he could always make passes like player B in the example.

Coaching of course depends on the group you work with. Find out for yourself the level of your team. For many players it is difficult enough to enlarge the field at the moment their team gets possession of the ball. Coaching starts with basics and the first thing you do when your team is in possession is spread out.

25. 5 vs 5 with 2 wall passers

12 players

The two teams play five versus five. Two wall passers at each short side can touch the ball once and help the team in possession. (To make it easier, let the wall passer touch the ball twice, or even more). The object is to maintain possession. Points can be scored with either a certain amount of passes made or a pass from one wall passer to the other. Notice: at Ajax they often play this game without a point system.

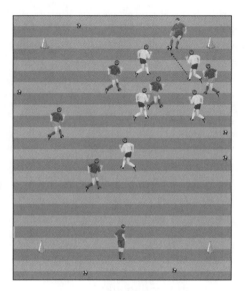

In order to maintain possession there needs to be good movement without the ball. Call for the ball after an action the other way and there should be a lot of coaching (especially from the wall passers). The team in possession should try to open up the field with a long ball to make it easier to create more time and space.

However, this drill is maybe even more important for the players who are not in possession. They have to try to win the ball and wait for the correct moment to do so. So coaching actually depends on what the coach's goal is, what does he want to achieve?

The diagram shows the correct moment to put pressure on the ball.

This drill can be used for many reasons and it's a good one for all levels. For Ajax, it is a good one for the extension of the warm up, but for most lower levels, this is what you practice on during the learning phase. Make this drill as easy as you want, by enlarging the field, or by playing 5vs4.

26. Positional play during a fanatical game

16 players and a goalie

An 8 v. 8 match on a small field, normal soccer rules apply. One team scores in the big goal with the goalie, the other team tries to score in one of the two small goals.

Depending on the objective of the practice, you can coach on tactics perfectly. At Ajax, however, this game is often used as a final test.

Sometimes a coach wants to see whether his players are focused on the next match. Maybe the team will play a match the next day. Of course he does not want to wear the team out. It's just about accuracy.

This drill is an ideal pre-game drill. Play it in two halves of ten minutes or even less and have a big break between the halves. Because the field is so small, there are lots of "duels", so players have to give everything they have. Concentration has to be one hundred percent to be able to play good positional play.

The drill is also good at all levels and for all occasions on a larger field. Put the two goals half way on the other side of the pitch and you can work on positional play perfectly. It's especially good to team the attackers against the defenders.

27. Are you focused?

9 players and 1 goalkeeper

6 players and 1 goalkeeper try to stay in possession of the ball in the penalty box. 3 players try to win the ball. As soon as they have it, they can score on goal. If the ball goes out of play, the coach tosses a new ball to the team that should have possession.

A match takes about 3 to 4 minutes, followed by a rest of 2 to 3 minutes. Play three series. Which three players score the most goals?

This is a good drill to test the skills of your goalie under pressure. But the most important coaching aspect is the moment the six players lose the ball and the three players win it. Players have to be focused at all times in these situations and it is good practice for a match. If players forget to transition, or even if it takes longer than a split second, teams at the level of Ajax' opponents will not fail to score. Matches are decided at these moments and this drill works on that mental aspect.

At a lower level the drill is also good to practice the positional play of the six players and the goalie and for the cooperation of the three players. When should they try to win the ball? How should they cooperate? The three players should always chase the ball together and try to wait for a moment when the six pass a weak ball to one of the sides, then immediately put pressure on the ball and one or two sides. If the three chase smartly, the player that puts pressure on the ball puts pressure on one side of the player that is in possession. That way, that player is forced to play the ball to the other side, where hopefully another chaser is on time to intercept his pass.

28. 4 v 4 with 3 wall players

11 players

This time the teams try to maintain possession during a 4 v 4 with three wall players. Two of the wall players are positioned at the long sides and one is stationed in the middle. The players can touch the ball a maximum of two times, but they have to try to do it in one pass. Ten passes for one team is a point. Play the match on time or until one of the teams has four points. The pitch is not very big (25 by 15 yards), but should be larger at lower levels.

Coach on movement without the ball and finding the third man. In particular, the wall player in the center should try to constantly open up. The most important thing is that the players in possession create space.

These drills are my favorites, even though I wouldn't play them with a two touch maximum. You can coach on everything you like, which is a reason to use them often. Players recognize the drill and the coach can just choose the problem he would like to work on.

29. 7 v 7 with a neutral player

15 players and two goalkeepers

A regular match of 7 v 7, played on one half of the field. Both teams can use the neutral player as soon as they are in possession of the ball. The neutral player can also score, so as soon as one team is in possession, it is 8 v 7.
The duration of the match depends on the point in the season. Mostly it is halves of 10-15 minutes.

Coaching should be on finding the extra man, but of course it depends on what you want to coach on. You can coach on every soccer problem you like, from the way you want to put pressure on the ball to finding the third man in possession or even on transitions.

Crowd favorite Jari Litmanen was often the neutral player in these kinds of games. That way, it was more like 9 v 7, because Litmanen is probably one of the world's best players at finding the right moment to get in possession, followed by sending the right pass to the right person. The neutral player is always the player who has the most space to make actions. Working with neutral players is a perfect way to help players see when they have to call for the ball and how to create space for themselves.

30. 5vs5 Tournament

15 players plus 2 or 3 goalkeepers

Three teams of five play a tournament. Every time a team scores, it gets a point and it plays again. The team that loses goes out. The first team to win five matches (the first team to score five goals) wins. After one of the teams has won, the other two teams finish play until one of them also reaches five.

If a team loses a match the players can rest, or collect balls.

Both teams play in the same formation, so there are 1 v1s all over the pitch. Movement without the ball is very important. And of course the coach has to make sure that there is an absolute winning spirit, since this is a tournament. Try to be like Tonny Bruins Slot. Motivate the players constantly and sometimes take a strange refereeing decision to get the adrenaline of the players to a top level. The Ajax assistant coach always tries to get a lot of suspense in the game. A team that is winning a lot does not have to count on a good referee.

At Ajax, this tournament was often used to give the players that did not play on the night or day before some extra practice. The players that did play would already be resting, while the others were sweating.

31. 2 v 2 with two goalies

4 (or 6) players and 2 (or 3) goalkeepers

A regular match of 2 v 2 on a small field (20 by 15 yards). The goalkeepers aren't allowed to score. As soon as one of the two players is in possession, they can't pass the ball back to the goalkeeper anymore. If the ball goes out of play, one of the goalkeepers immediately throws  another ball in. Matches take 2 minutes, with 1.5 minutes rest.

This is actually a drill to build up stamina. Especially with youth teams there are a couple of things to coach on. The moment to call for the ball is one. A player should always create space for himself and then make an action to call for the ball at the right time.
Also you can coach on dummying and defending. In this game it is important to shoot as soon as possible, so defenders have to defend at very close range (just like they would in their own penalty area). Always tell the defenders to stand on the front part of their feet and to bend their knees. This way, they are able to move quickly.

There were days at Ajax that only 8 or even less players joined practice. This happened when there were international games and some injury problems. The players had to play this drill more than once, because it's an excellent drill to stay in shape. It is very intense and fun. Normally there would be three teams, who would each play the other two teams a couple of times. Teams were always picked with special attention. For instance: Brazilians with Brazilians, blond Dutch players together, African players together, small players, etcetera. In a match of two minutes a score of 3-2 is not unusual.

32. Practicing the system

x players and a goalkeeper

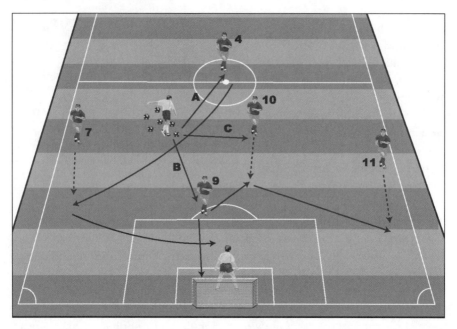

The coach has a supply of balls and starts each play. The goal of every play is to score as soon as possible, but always playing from the player's position and practicing different ways of attacks.

Coach passes ball back to number 4, who either opens to number 7 or 11. 7 or 11 can make a wall pass with 10 or 9, then go into space to give the cross. 9 and 10 try to score. 7 and 11 do not necessarily have to make the wall pass, they can also reach the goal line by dribbling. Coach passes to number 9, who tries to score, or makes a short combination with 10 to score. Number 9 (the central striker) can also pass the ball to a winger, who always have to move.

Coach passes the ball to number 10, who can try to score, or set up an attack by passing back to number 4. Or he makes a combination with number 9.

A couple of things are important with this drill. For instance, the movement of the wingers (7 and 11). They have to make moves before receiving the ball. They can do that by first going away and then coming into the ball and calling for it.

Also important is the movement of the two strikers. If a winger has the ball, they have to choose their position in front of the goal. One usually goes near post, the other one goes to the far post. They should not be in the same line with the ball.

The coach also pays attention to the distance between the numbers 9 and 10. It should be around 10-15 yards, before one receives the ball.

This drill can be used at the start of the season. Use defenders to make it more difficult.

33. Practicing the system (2)

7 or 8 players, 1 or 2 goalies

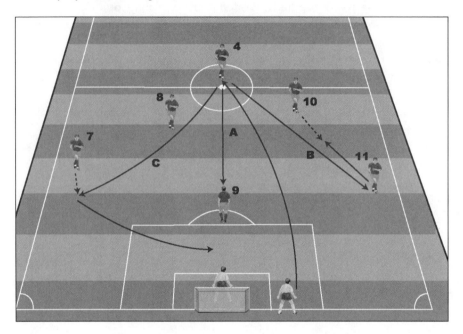

Again different kinds of attacks are practiced without opponents. This time using the second system, a system that Ajax played very often last season, especially in European matches. The system actually contains two number 10s, who both have a more defensive role than a single number 10 would have.

Every attack begins after number 4 has received a long ball from the goalie. An attack should take a maximum of five seconds from the moment number 4 has controlled the ball.
Number 4 passes to the striker, number 9. The striker either shoots imme- diately or passes the ball back to number 8 or number 10, depending on who calls for the ball.

Number 4 passes to one of the wingers. The winger either makes a wall pass with number 8 or 10 or sends in a cross himself. The moment he makes the cross number 9 should be at the near post, while one mid- fielder and the other winger should be at the far post. It is important in this system that the winger does not have to reach the goal line before making his cross. He sends in the cross at or even before the 16-yard line. That way he can immediately pick up his defensive role if the ball is lost. In this system everything has to be done at full speed, for most attacks are actually counter attacks.

Number 4 passes to a winger. The moment the pass is given the left or right back rushes forward. The winger passes the ball to him and the back sends in the cross. Again the positional play of the attackers at the moment of the cross is very important.

The role of the coach is huge in this drill; attacks should follow each other at high speed.

The roles of the left and right back are crucial. Ajax is very lucky to have players like Hatem Trabelsi, John O'Brien and Maxwell who perform those roles perfectly.

34. Koeman's cooling down drill

3 or 4 wingers, 8+ players and one (or two) goalkeepers

Player A gives a short pass to B. He opens with a high cross to a winger (who was already sprinting). The winger can make a wall pass to player D if necessary, or player D can pick up the ball and pass to the winger if the high cross by B was not good.
The winger crosses to players A and B, who try to score as quickly as possible.

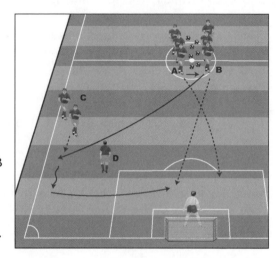

Every time a different winger is player D, who actually does not have an important role at all and is just there in case the first cross is not good.

Coach on how to give a high cross and also on the movement of the two strikers A and B, one to the near post, one to the far post and they should not be in one line with the ball at the moment of the cross.

This drill was used a lot, at least two times a week last season, and especially at the end of a heavy practice. Usually it took about 10-20 minutes to get the players to cool down. After 5-10 minutes the right wingers make place for left wingers. Andy van der Meyde always proved to be superb in this drill, which might have helped him earn his transfer to Italian side Internazionale.

At lower levels, this drill is ideal to improve the technique of crossing. And because it does not take a lot of energy, it is perfect for a warm season start to work on the skills of the players.

35. A practice to recover

6 players (or more)

The day after a big match, it is of course impossible to train with maximum intensity. Usually, the players who did play will train for only a short time on the field. And then only to help their bodies recover by doing some low intensity drills.

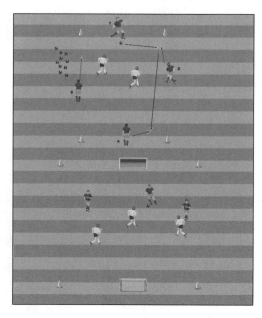

In a normal week, when Ajax would play on a Sunday, the players would have a day off on Tuesday. However, with all these international games in Champions League or for national teams and also cup matches on Wednesdays, the day off was often dropped. Soccer players are lazy? There were runs of 25 days without a day off!

A recovery practice usually starts with an extended warm-up and some fun drills with the ball, and always on very small pitches. In this example, the players play 4 vs 2. There are no points to be gained and there is no coaching. After a ten or twelve minutes, the players switch to a little game of 3 vs 3, again on a small field. Again nobody counts points and especially when the match of the day before was won, there will be a lot of laughing.

Zlatan Ibrahimovic was one of the kings of the recovery practice. Now he had time to show all his tricks, without anybody being worried about him losing the ball. His skills are incredible and even though he had a tough start in Amsterdam, many people are sure the tall young Swedish striker will become one of the world's top players.

Practices for players who are recovering from an injury usually involve a lot of running and a lot of passing and shooting. The players almost never play a game and there is never actually something like 1 v 1 involved, except at the very end of the recovery period. If you're lucky, you have a special coach who helps players to return after an injury. For those who don't, here are six examples of practices. Oh yes, there is not much coaching here, just a lot of doing.

36a. Recovery from an injury

2-4 players

Two players in the middle are both in possession of a ball. They start passing it to the coaches. In the example, player A passes the ball to player C, calls for the ball again, gets it back, dribbles a little, then passes it to player D, calls for the ball again, gets it back etc. Meanwhile player B does the same.
You can also do this with headers.

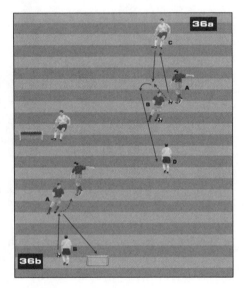

The drill takes about two minutes with one minute rest (or the players can rotate). If only two players are recovering from an injury, the two players at the sides could be players that are fit or coaches.

36b. Recovery from an injury

2 to 4 players

Player A sprints towards the ball. Player B passes the ball, player A finishes on the small goal. Then he runs around the goal, sprints and finishes another pass. After ten shots, the finishers get at least a one minute rest.

37a. Recovery from an injury

2 to 4 players

Two players play 1 v. 1 on a small field. The two players in front of the goal are not goalies but wall players. They can help the defender if he is in possession, but they cannot defend themselves. A match takes 90 seconds, followed by 90 seconds of rest.

37b. Recovery from an injury

2 to 4 players

This time the players practice the long ball (but not too long, since they are recovering). The distance between them is about 25 yards. Player A passes to player B, who makes a wall pass with player C, then B passes back to player A, who makes a wall pass with D, followed by a pass from A to B, etcetera.

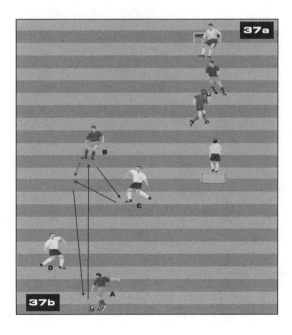

38a. Recovery from an injury

2 to 4 players

One coach passes to the midfielder, who sends in a cross to the striker. He prepares the ball for number 10, who finishes. One series of ten shots. The shot should be at full power, but only do this when the player is ready for it.

38b. Recovery from an injury

1 goal keeper, 3 players

Player A makes a wall pass with player B and then tries to finish on goal. Immediately after his shot, there is a cross from the side and Player A has to finish that one as well with one touch. Ten finishes, three series.

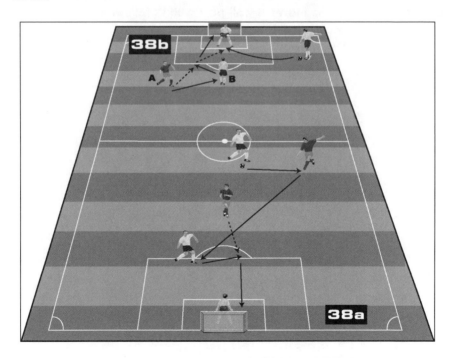

39a. A goalkeeper under pressure

2 goalkeepers

The coach passes the ball to goalkeeper A. As soon as he passes, goalkeeper B puts pressure on goalkeeper A, who tries to score in the small goal.
Play five times to the left and five times to the right.
Play a match between the goalies. Who scores the most goals?

The goalkeeper should try to do this with two touches. Also, he should try to score in the left goal by shooting with his left foot, while scoring in the right goal by shooting with his right foot. Of course he should also try to put his body between the ball and the opponent and... **NEVER TAKE ANY RISKS**.

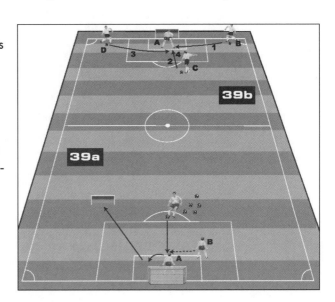

39b. A drill for goalkeepers

4 goalkeepers (or 1 goalkeeper and 3 players)

Goalkeeper A is in goal. Goalkeeper B passes a high ball to him with his right foot. A should try to stop this shot. Then C shoots on goal, followed by a pass from D with his left foot and another shot by C. After five turns goalkeepers rotate.
It is possible to make this drill more difficult by putting a striker near the goal who puts pressure on the goalkeeper during the crosses.

Ajax had an unlucky year with goalies. Most of the time at least two of them were injured. At one point Bogdan Lobont, Maarten Stekelenburg, Joey Didulica and Henk Timmer were all fit. Then goalie coach Wil Coort came up with this drill to practice passing with left and right, shooting and of course goalkeeping with four goalies in one drill.

40a. A tough day for goalkeepers

5 goalkeepers

On a very small field the five goalies play 4 v. 1. The four players can only touch the ball once. The one in the middle has to dive at the ball and if he gets to one, he has to get up and try to score in one of the two goals. The goalkeeper in the middle can't win

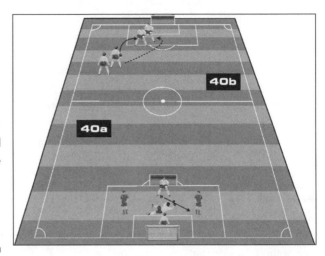

the ball with his feet. He has to dive.

Goalkeepers rotate after 45 seconds. Who scores the most goals?

When Edwin van der Sar joined Ajax for a couple of practices just to stay in shape, the five goalkeepers got really tired with this drill. It is a very good drill for younger goalies, as they learn how to dive.

40b. Throwing

4 or more goalkeepers

Goalkeeper A throws the ball to B. B catches the ball and throws it to C, who throws to D. The goalkeepers follow their throw, so A becomes B, etc.

Coach the goalkeeper. It's no coincidence that the throws are towards the side. A goalkeeper should always try to avoid playing balls through the center of the field because of the immediate danger.

This is an easy warm-up for goalkeepers. Play it three minutes to the right and three minutes to the left.

Ronald Koeman's top ten most used drills, 2002-2003:

(based on my counting)

drill 1, Ronald Koeman's famous warm up

drill 5, Improve the pass with your laces

drill 22, Positional play and technique, 4v 2

drill 34, Koeman's cooling down drill

drill 32, Practicing the system

drill 33, Practicing the system (2)

drill 12, Conditioning with a fanatical match

drill 13, A great shooting and conditioning drill

drill 24, Finding the third man

drill 14, Heavy work on conditioning and technique

Smink's top five most used drills for U-9:

drill 7, How to shoot?

drill 11, Finishing and conditioning (but now the coaching moment is on the technique and not on conditioning).

drill 17, Passing, dribbling, dummying, scoring! (And defending!)

drill 12, Conditioning with a fanatical match (here the coaching is also on technique and not on conditioning).

drill 1, Ronald Koeman's famous warming up

Smink's top five most used drills for U-14:

drill 22, Positional play and technique, 4 v 2

drill 21, Positional play, 4 v 4 and four wall passers

drill 27, are you focused?

drill 23, More positional play

drill 14, Heavy work on conditioning and technique

Smink's top five most used drills for U-19:

drill 1, Ronald Koeman's famous warming up

drill 24, Finding the third man

drill 13, A great shooting and conditioning drill

drill 27, are you focused?

drill 34, Koeman's cooling down drill

Last season (2002-2003) Ajax Amsterdam reached the quarter finals of the Champions League. They were eliminated by a last minute goal from Felipe Inzaghi of AC Milan who went on to win the famous trophy. Ajax finished second in the Dutch league and reached the semi finals of the Dutch Cup. They did not win a prize, but one thing was clear to everyone: Ajax was back at the top of European football.

Jorrit Smink (27) was a sports journalist for the Amsterdam newspaper Het Parool and followed the development of the young team the whole year through. He had a daily column in the newspaper, but also wrote down all the drills that were given by coach Ronald Koeman.

In this book, Smink, who is currently studying for his UEFA B soccer coaching license, explains the drills that Ajax uses. This book is about the way Smink saw them reaching for the top. It's a unique collection of fifty drills used by Ajax Amsterdam during their Champions League season. Smink explains the drills and also translates them, so coaches at all levels can use them.